CLARINET

101 JAZZ SO

Available for
FLUTE, CLARINET, ALTO SAX, TENOR SAX, TRUMPET,
HORN, TROMBONE, VIOLIN, VIOLA, CELLO

ISBN 978-1-4950-2337-8

HAL•LEONARD®
CORPORATION

7777 W. BLUEMOUND RD. P.O. BOX 13819 MILWAUKEE, WI 53213

Visit Hal Leonard Online at
www.halleonard.com

CONTENTS

4 All of Me

5 All the Things You Are

6 April in Paris

7 Autumn in New York

8 Autumn Leaves

9 Bewitched

10 Beyond the Sea

11 The Blue Room

12 Blue Skies

13 Bluesette

14 Body and Soul

15 But Beautiful

16 Can't Help Lovin' Dat Man

17 Caravan

18 Charade

19 Cheek to Cheek

20 Come Rain or Come Shine

21 Dancing on the Ceiling

22 Dearly Beloved

23 Do Nothin' Till You Hear from Me

24 Don't Get Around Much Anymore

25 Dreamsville

26 Falling in Love with Love

27 A Fine Romance

28 Fly Me to the Moon (In Other Words)

29 Georgia on My Mind

30 Here's That Rainy Day

31 Here's to Life

32 Honeysuckle Rose

33 How Deep Is the Ocean (How High Is the Sky)

34 How Insensitive (Insensatez)

35 I Can't Get Started

36 I Could Write a Book

37 I Got It Bad and That Ain't Good

38 I'll Remember April

39 I'm Beginning to See the Light

40 I've Got the World on a String

41 If I Were a Bell

42 Imagination

43 In a Sentimental Mood

44 In the Wee Small Hours of the Morning

45 Indiana (Back Home Again in Indiana)

46 Isn't It Romantic?

47 It Could Happen to You

48 It Don't Mean a Thing (If It Ain't Got That Swing)

49 It Might as Well Be Spring

50 The Lady Is a Tramp

51 Lazy River

52 Let There Be Love

53 Like Someone in Love

54 Little Girl Blue

55 Long Ago (And Far Away)

56 Lover, Come Back to Me

57 Lullaby of Birdland

58 Lullaby of the Leaves

59 Manhattan

60 Meditation (Meditação)

61 Midnight Sun

62 Misty

63 Mood Indigo

64 Moonlight in Vermont

65 More Than You Know

66 My Heart Stood Still

67 My Old Flame

68 My One and Only Love

69 My Romance

70 My Ship

71 The Nearness of You

72 A Night in Tunisia

73 On Green Dolphin Street

74 One Note Samba (Samba de uma nota so)

75 Pick Yourself Up

76 Polka Dots and Moonbeams

77 Quiet Nights of Quiet Stars (Corcovado)

78 Satin Doll

79 Skylark

80 So Nice (Summer Samba)

81 Sophisticated Lady

82 Speak Low

83 Stella by Starlight

84 Stompin' at the Savoy

85 Stormy Weather (Keeps Rainin' All the Time)

86 A Sunday Kind of Love

87 Tangerine

88 There's a Small Hotel

89 These Foolish Things (Remind Me of You)

90 The Things We Did Last Summer

91 This Can't Be Love

92 Thou Swell

93 Unforgettable

94 The Very Thought of You

95 Watch What Happens

96 Wave

97 The Way You Look Tonight

98 What'll I Do?

99 Willow Weep for Me

100 Witchcraft

101 Yesterdays

102 You Are Too Beautiful

103 You Brought a New Kind of Love to Me

104 You Don't Know What Love Is

ALL OF ME

CLARINET

Words and Music by SEYMOUR SIMONS
and GERALD MARKS

Moderately

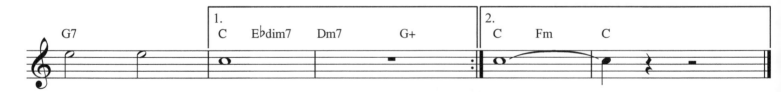

ALL THE THINGS YOU ARE

Clarinet

Lyrics by OSCAR HAMMERSTEIN II
Music by JEROME KERN

APRIL IN PARIS

Clarinet

Words by E.Y. "YIP" HARBURG
Music by VERNON DUKE

Moderately

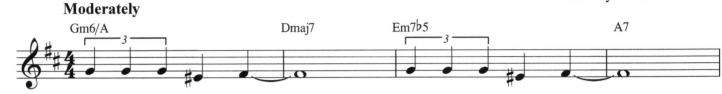

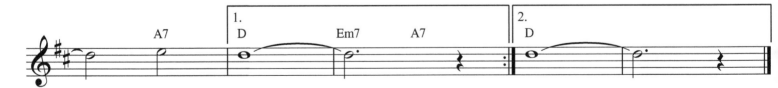

AUTUMN IN NEW YORK

Clarinet

Words and Music by
VERNON DUKE

AUTUMN LEAVES

Clarinet

English Lyric by JOHNNY MERCER
French Lyric by JACQUES PREVERT
Music by JOSEPH KOSMA

BEWITCHED

Clarinet

Words by LORENZ HART
Music by RICHARD RODGERS

BEYOND THE SEA

Lyrics by JACK LAWRENCE
Music by CHARLES TRENET and ALBERT LASRY
Original French Lyric to "La Mer" by CHARLES TRENET

CLARINET

THE BLUE ROOM

Clarinet

Words by LORENZ HART
Music by RICHARD RODGERS

BLUE SKIES

CLARINET

Words and Music by
IRVING BERLIN

BLUESETTE

CLARINET

Words by NORMAN GIMBEL
Music by JEAN THIELEMANS

BODY AND SOUL

Clarinet

Words by EDWARD HEYMAN,
ROBERT SOUR and FRANK EYTON
Music by JOHN GREEN

BUT BEAUTIFUL

Clarinet

Words by JOHNNY BURKE
Music by JIMMY VAN HEUSEN

CAN'T HELP LOVIN' DAT MAN

Clarinet

Lyrics by OSCAR HAMMERSTEIN II
Music by JEROME KERN

CARAVAN

Clarinet

Words and Music by DUKE ELLINGTON,
IRVING MILLS and JUAN TIZOL

CHARADE

Clarinet

By HENRY MANCINI

CHEEK TO CHEEK

CLARINET

Words and Music by
IRVING BERLIN

COME RAIN OR COME SHINE

Clarinet

Words by JOHNNY MERCER
Music by HAROLD ARLEN

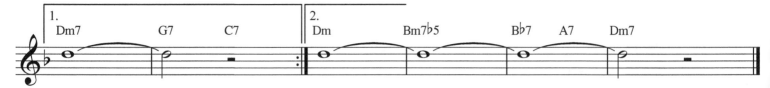

Dancing on the Ceiling

Words by LORENZ HART
Music by RICHARD RODGERS

Clarinet

DEARLY BELOVED

Clarinet

Music by JEROME KERN
Words by JOHNNY MERCER

DO NOTHIN' TILL YOU HEAR FROM ME

Clarinet

Words and Music by DUKE ELLINGTON
and BOB RUSSELL

DON'T GET AROUND MUCH ANYMORE

Clarinet

Words and Music by DUKE ELLINGTON
and BOB RUSSELL

DREAMSVILLE

Clarinet

By HENRY MANCINI

FALLING IN LOVE WITH LOVE

Clarinet

Words by LORENZ HART
Music by RICHARD RODGERS

A FINE ROMANCE

Clarinet

Words by DOROTHY FIELDS
Music by JEROME KERN

FLY ME TO THE MOON
(In Other Words)

Clarinet

Words and Music by
BART HOWARD

Georgia on My Mind

Words by STUART GORRELL
Music by HOAGY CARMICHAEL

Clarinet

HERE'S THAT RAINY DAY

Clarinet

Words by JOHNNY BURKE
Music by JIMMY VAN HEUSEN

HERE'S TO LIFE

Clarinet

Music by ARTIE BUTLER
Lyrics by PHYLLIS MOLINARY

HONEYSUCKLE ROSE

Clarinet

Words by ANDY RAZAF
Music by THOMAS "FATS" WALLER

HOW DEEP IS THE OCEAN

(How High Is the Sky)

Clarinet

Words and Music by
IRVING BERLIN

HOW INSENSITIVE
(Insensatez)

Clarinet

Music by ANTONIO CARLOS JOBIM
Original Words by VINICIUS DE MORAES
English Words by NORMAN GIMBEL

Medium Bossa Nova

I CAN'T GET STARTED

Clarinet

Words by IRA GERSHWIN
Music by VERNON DUKE

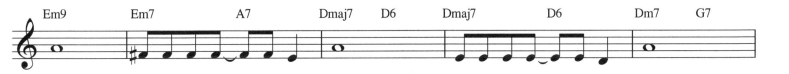

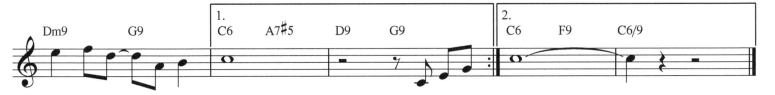

I COULD WRITE A BOOK

Clarinet

Words by LORENZ HART
Music by RICHARD RODGERS

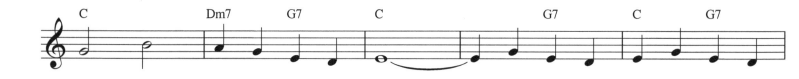

I GOT IT BAD AND THAT AIN'T GOOD

Clarinet

Words by PAUL FRANCIS WEBSTER
Music by DUKE ELLINGTON

I'LL REMEMBER APRIL

CLARINET

Words and Music by PAT JOHNSTON,
DON RAYE AND GENE DE PAUL

Moderately

I'M BEGINNING TO SEE THE LIGHT

Clarinet

Words and Music by DON GEORGE, JOHNNY HODGES,
DUKE ELLINGTON and HARRY JAMES

Medium Bounce

I'VE GOT THE WORLD ON A STRING

Clarinet

Words by TED KOEHLER
Music by HAROLD ARLEN

IF I WERE A BELL

CLARINET

By FRANK LOESSER

IMAGINATION

Clarinet

Words by JOHNNY BURKE
Music by JIMMY VAN HEUSEN

IN A SENTIMEMTAL MOOD

Clarinet

By Duke Ellington

IN THE WEE SMALL HOURS OF THE MORNING

Clarinet

Words by BOB HILLIARD
Music by DAVID MANN

INDIANA
(Back Home Again in Indiana)

Clarinet

Words by BALLARD MacDONALD
Music by JAMES F. HANLEY

ISN'T IT ROMANTIC?

Clarinet

Words by LORENZ HART
Music by RICHARD RODGERS

IT COULD HAPPEN TO YOU

Clarinet

Words by JOHNNY BURKE
Music by JAMES VAN HEUSEN

IT DON'T MEAN A THING
(If It Ain't Got That Swing)

Clarinet

Words and Music by DUKE ELLINGTON
and IRVING MILLS

Fast Swing

IT MIGHT AS WELL BE SPRING

Clarinet

Lyrics by OSCAR HAMMERSTEIN II
Music by RICHARD RODGERS

Moderately

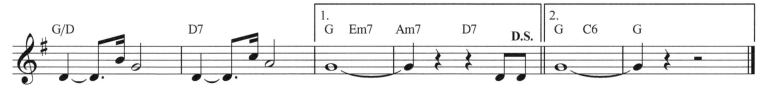

THE LADY IS A TRAMP

CLARINET

Words by LORENZ HART
Music by RICHARD RODGERS

Moderately

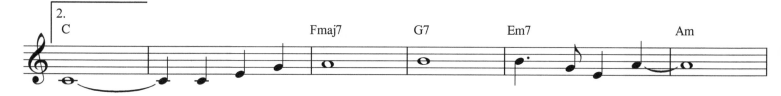

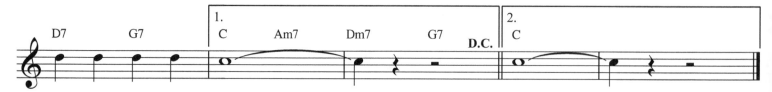

LAZY RIVER

Clarinet

Words and Music by HOAGY CARMICHAEL
and SIDNEY ARODIN

LET THERE BE LOVE

CLARINET

Lyric by IAN GRANT
Music by LIONEL RAND

LIKE SOMEONE IN LOVE

Words by JOHNNY BURKE
Music by JIMMY VAN HEUSEN

Clarinet

LITTLE GIRL BLUE

Clarinet

Words by LORENZ HART
Music by RICHARD RODGERS

LONG AGO (AND FAR AWAY)

Clarinet

Words by IRA GERSHWIN
Music by JEROME KERN

Moderately slow

LOVER, COME BACK TO ME

Clarinet

Lyrics by OSCAR HAMMERSTEIN II
Music by SIGMUND ROMBERG

Moderately

LULLABY OF BIRDLAND

Clarinet

Words by GEORGE DAVID WEISS
Music by GEORGE SHEARING

LULLABY OF THE LEAVES

Clarinet

Words by JOE YOUNG
Music by BERNICE PETKERE

MANHATTAN

Clarinet

Words by LORENZ HART
Music by RICHARD RODGERS

MEDITATION
(Meditação)

Clarinet

Music by ANTONIO CARLOS JOBIM
Original Words by NEWTON MENDONÇA
English Words by NORMAN GIMBEL

MIDNIGHT SUN

Clarinet

Words and Music by LIONEL HAMPTON,
SONNY BURKE and JOHNNY MERCER

MISTY

Clarinet

Music by ERROLL GARNER

MOOD INDIGO

Clarinet

Words and Music by DUKE ELLINGTON,
IRVING MILLS and ALBANY BIGARD

Moderately slow

MOONLIGHT IN VERMONT

Clarinet

Words by JOHN BLACKBURN
Music by KARL SUESSDORF

MORE THAN YOU KNOW

Clarinet

Words by WILLIAM ROSE and EDWARD ELISCU
Music by VINCENT YOUMANS

MY HEART STOOD STILL

Clarinet

Words by LORENZ HART
Music by RICHARD RODGERS

MY OLD FLAME

Clarinet

Words and Music by ARTHUR JOHNSTON
and SAM COSLOW

MY ONE AND ONLY LOVE

Clarinet

Words by ROBERT MELLIN
Music by GUY WOOD

MY ROMANCE

Clarinet

Words by LORENZ HART
Music by RICHARD RODGERS

MY SHIP

Clarinet

Words by IRA GERSHWIN
Music by KURT WEILL

THE NEARNESS OF YOU

Clarinet

Words by NED WASHINGTON
Music by HOAGY CARMICHAEL

A NIGHT IN TUNISIA

Clarinet

By JOHN "DIZZY" GILLESPIE
and FRANK PAPARELLI

Moderately fast Swing

ON GREEN DOLPHIN STREET

Clarinet

Lyrics by NED WASHINGTON
Music by BRONISLAU KAPER

ONE NOTE SAMBA
(Samba de uma nota so)

Clarinet

Original Lyrics by NEWTON MENDONÇA
English Lyrics by ANTONIO CARLOS JOBIM
Music by ANTONIO CARLOS JOBIM

Medium Bossa Nova

PICK YOURSELF UP

Clarinet

Words by DOROTHY FIELDS
Music by JEROME KERN

POLKA DOTS AND MOONBEAMS

Clarinet

Words by JOHNNY BURKE
Music by JIMMY VAN HEUSEN

QUIET NIGHTS OF QUIET STARS
(Corcovado)

Clarinet

English Words by GENE LEES
Original Words and Music by ANTONIO CARLOS JOBIM

Medium Bossa Nova

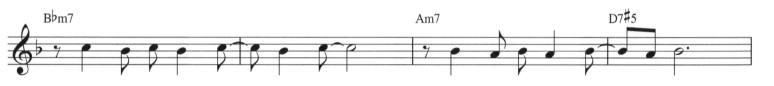

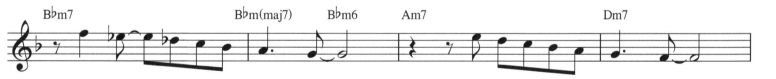

SATIN DOLL

Clarinet

By DUKE ELLINGTON

SKYLARK

Clarinet

Words by JOHNNY MERCER
Music by HOAGY CARMICHAEL

Moderate Swing

SO NICE
(Summer Samba)

CLARINET

Original Words and Music by MARCOS VALLE
and PAULO SERGIO VALLE
English Words by NORMAN GIMBEL

Medium Bossa Nova

SOPHISTICATED LADY

Clarinet

Words and Music by DUKE ELLINGTON,
IRVING MILLS and MITCHELL PARISH

SPEAK LOW

Clarinet

Words by OGDEN NASH
Music by KURT WEILL

STELLA BY STARLIGHT

Words by NED WASHINGTON
Music by VICTOR YOUNG

Clarinet

STOMPIN' AT THE SAVOY

Clarinet

By BENNY GOODMAN,
EDGAR SAMPSON and CHICK WEBB

STORMY WEATHER
(Keeps Rainin' All the Time)

Clarinet

Lyric by TED KOEHLER
Music by HAROLD ARLEN

A Sunday Kind of Love

Words and Music by LOUIS PRIMA, ANITA NYE LEONARD,
STANLEY RHODES and BARBARA BELLE

Clarinet

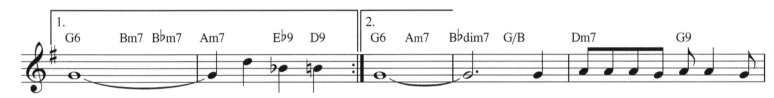

TANGERINE

Words by JOHNNY MERCER
Music by VICTOR SCHERTZINGER

Clarinet

THERE'S A SMALL HOTEL

CLARINET

Words by LORENZ HART
Music by RICHARD RODGERS

THESE FOOLISH THINGS (REMIND ME OF YOU)

Clarinet

Words by HOLT MARVELL
Music by JACK STRACHEY

THE THINGS WE DID LAST SUMMER

Clarinet

Words by SAMMY CAHN
Music by JULE STYNE

Moderate Swing

This Can't Be Love

Clarinet

Words by LORENZ HART
Music by RICHARD RODGERS

THOU SWELL

Clarinet

Words by LORENZ HART
Music by RICHARD RODGERS

UNFORGETTABLE

Clarinet

Words and Music by
IRVING GORDON

THE VERY THOUGHT OF YOU

Clarinet

Words and Music by
RAY NOBLE

WATCH WHAT HAPPENS

Music by MICHEL LEGRAND
Original French Text by JACQUES DEMY
English Lyrics by NORMAN GIMBEL

Clarinet

WAVE

CLARINET

Words and Music by
ANTONIO CARLOS JOBIM

Medium Bossa Nova

THE WAY YOU LOOK TONIGHT

Clarinet

Words by DOROTHY FIELDS
Music by JEROME KERN

WHAT'LL I DO

CLARINET

Words and Music by
IRVING BERLIN

WILLOW WEEP FOR ME

Clarinet

Words and Music by
ANN RONELL

WITCHCRAFT

Clarinet

Music by CY COLEMAN
Lyrics by CAROLYN LEIGH

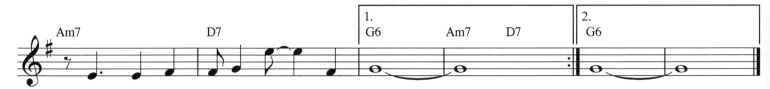

YESTERDAYS

Clarinet

Words by OTTO HARBACH
Music by JEROME KERN

YOU ARE TOO BEAUTIFUL

Clarinet

Words by LORENZ HART
Music by RICHARD RODGERS

Slowly, with expression

YOU BROUGHT A NEW KIND OF LOVE TO ME

Clarinet

Words and Music by SAMMY FAIN,
IRVING KAHAL and PIERRE NORMAN

Medium Swing

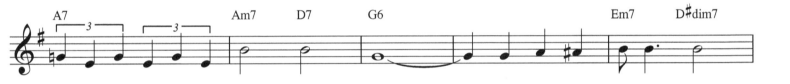

YOU DON'T KNOW WHAT LOVE IS

Clarinet

Words and Music by DON RAYE
and GENE DePAUL